BICYCLING BASICS

by Tim and Glenda Wilhelm

Illustrated by

Art Seiden

Plus Photographs

Created and Produced by

Arvid Knudsen

PRENTICE-HALL, Inc.

Englewood Cliffs, N.J.

DEDICATION
To two Moms and a Pop who encouraged each of us to do more than spin our wheels.

Acknowledgement and thanks is hereby given
to the Columbia Bicycle Manufacturing
Company for the use of its resource materials.

Other Sports Basics Books in Series

Book design by Arvid Knudsen

Printed in the United States of America   .J

Prentice-Hall International, Inc., London
Prentice-Hall of Australia, Pty. Ltd., North Sydney
Prentice-Hall of Canada, Ltd., Toronto
Prentice-Hall of India Private Ltd., New Delhi
Prentice-Hall of Japan, Inc., Tokyo
Prentice-Hall of Southeast Asia Pte. Ltd., Singapore
Whitehall Books Limited, Wellington, New Zealand

10 9 8 7 6 5 4 3 2 1

Library of Congress Cataloging in Publication Data

Wilhelm, Tim.
    Bicycling basics.

    Summary: Traces the history of bicycling and
describes the modern bicycle and its parts. Includes
advice on buying a bicycle, learning to ride correctly
and safely, touring, and bicycle racing.
    Includes index.

    1. Cycling--Juvenile literature. 2. Bicycle touring--
Juvenile literature. [1. Bicycles and bicycling]
I. Wilhelm, Glenda. II. Seiden, Art, ill. III. Title.
GV1043.5.W54   796.6   82-7628
ISBN 0-13-077958-X   Rev.

CONTENTS

4806

Preface

Once you have your own bicycle, you have taken a first step into the adult world of transportation. It will be several years perhaps before you sit behind the wheel of an automobile, yet you will be riding your bicycle on roads and highways along with drivers who have had years of experience. You will be expected to know and follow the rules of the road that govern every driver, yet many of them will either not even see you or not consider you a "real" member of traffic.

It is up to you to be a responsible and careful cyclist. We hope this book will help you to learn about your bicycle, its history, and its role as a vehicle on the very real roads of your neighborhood and city or town. Even more than all of that, as you master the skills of cycling, we hope you will find a freedom of movement and joy in traveling whether you ride around the block or —someday—around the world.

Tim & Glenda Wilhelm

JOE BREEZE AND MONTE WARD ENJOY RIDING THEIR RITCHEY
MOUNTAIN BIKES IN THE ROUGH BACKCOUNTRY NEAR FAIRFAX,
CALIFORNIA. MOUNTAIN BIKES OR CRUISERS ARE GREAT
FOR OFF-ROAD TOURING OR RACING.
(Photo courtesy of Wende Cragg Photo)

THE DRAISINE WAS INVENTED
BY A GERMAN FORESTER IN 1817
TO RIDE ON HIS PATROLS
THROUGH THE WOODS. IT WAS
RIDDEN BY PUSHING AND
COASTING AS ON A SCOOTER.

1 | A SHORT HISTORY OF THE BICYCLE

The bicycle was invented a little at a time by many different people. It took 100 years for it to look and operate anything like a modern bicycle. In 1790 a Frenchman named Comte de Sivrac put wheels on a wooden horse-shaped frame. People, calling it a "hobbyhorse," sat on the frame and pushed themselves along with their feet. They thought it was great fun but a little dangerous, because there was no way to steer it. The hobbyhorse quickly became popular in other countries of Europe.

In 1839 a blacksmith in Scotland put cranks on the rear wheel of a hobbyhorse. That was the first true bicycle, because a rider had to balance and could turn the wheels without pushing along on the ground.

Some say the bicycle wasn't really a bicycle until it had pedals. In 1861, 70 years after the first hobbyhorse, Henry and Pierre Michaux attached pedals to the front wheel of one in their Paris coach and buggy workshop. With pedals

the rider turned the wheel directly with his feet, and the modern bicycle was born. The Michaux brothers called their invention a *velocipede*, Latin for "fast of foot." And fast it was.

Then something strange happened to the way a bicycle looked. Inventors knew that the bigger the wheel, the faster a bike could go. In England, James Starley designed a "highwheeler" with a huge front wheel and a tiny back wheel. It could go from 14 to 20 miles per hour, but the rider had a hard time balancing. The highwheeler was the first all-metal bicycle with spokes on the wheels and solid rubber tires.

People in America wanted to ride the English highwheeler, so Colonel Albert Pope brought some over the ocean with him to sell here. They proved so popular that he began building highwheelers in his own factory. He became the first big manufacturer of bicycles in America and used many new designs with different metals. He also led the fight for good roads. Highwheelers could go very fast, but crashed easily. The big front wheel would stop suddenly when it hit a rock or even a chicken or dog. The rider then "took a header," flying over the handlebars into the bushes or onto the road. It was as important to know how to fall as it was to know how to ride.

By 1885 the bicycle once again had two wheels that were the same size. Safer to ride than highwheelers, the "safety" cycle looked much like bicycles of today. More comfortable and easier to ride, safety cycles soon had coaster brakes, air-filled tires, chain-driven rear wheels, and frames made of metal tubing. People no longer had to worry about taking a header off a highwheeler.

Inventions that were first used on bicycles were important later in developing both the automobile and the airplane. Air-filled tires were invented by John Dunlop for his son's bicycle in 1889. The Wright brothers built, repaired, and sold bicycles before they built gliders and airplanes. Their first air machine had many bicycle parts, and they used bicycles to test air flow and lift.

People in the late 1800s liked bicycles so much that they paid the equivalent of $1500 today for one. Even though the machines weighed more than 70 pounds, they were more convenient than having to feed and care for a horse. Two-, three-, and four-wheeled cycles were popular also, some with seats for more than one rider.

So many bicycles were built and sold by 1900 that workers put them together in long lines in factories, each worker putting together one small part of the whole bicycle. This was the begining of the assembly line—a new idea that changed American industry. The assembly line was used later by Henry Ford in making automobiles and is still used today.

As more people rode bicycles, cycling clubs and organizations worked hard to get better roads. As more roads were paved, bicycling became a way of life. Then the automobile was invented. It took over the roads that cyclists had fought hard to have built. By the early 1900s a bicycle was no longer the fastest way to get around.

During the last 100 years of the bicycle's 200-year history, it has become lighter, faster, better able to climb steep hills, and a more efficient, inexpensive way to travel. Many people think bicycles are better than automobiles, because they don't use gas and they help keep the rider healthy at the same time. It took a lot of people to invent the modern bicycle. For a lot of people, the bicycle is still a good way to get where they want to go.

9

2 | THE MODERN BICYCLE AND ITS PARTS

The bicycle takes less energy to operate than any other kind of transportation invented by man. It is more efficient than an airplane, a rocket, an automobile, or a train. It travels farther on fewer calories than a dolphin gliding through the ocean or a bird flying through the air.

How does a bicycle work? Everyone knows a bicycle moves when a rider turns the pedals. But then what happens? The pedals are attached to crank arms that turn the chain wheel, a metal wheel with teeth all around the edge. Look for these parts on the bicycle diagram. The teeth on the chain wheel hold and turn a chain that goes to the rear wheel and loops around a smaller toothed wheel called a cog. This cog turns the axle and the rear wheel. A freewheel device lets the wheel keep turning even though the rider stops pedaling for awhile.

There are several ways to stop a bicycle. Coaster brakes are used on many children's bicycles. The bike is stopped by pushing backward on the pedals. Caliper brakes are worked by hand levers and cables that pinch the wheel between metal arms with rubber pads. Most middle- and lightweight bicycles have caliper brakes. Hub and disc brakes are operated by hand also, but work more like automobile brakes. They are inside the wheel hub or on a disc outside it. They are used on heavy-duty bicycles, such as tandems (bicycles built for two riders) and bicycles built for hauling heavy loads.

BRAKES

CALIPER BRAKES ARE FOUND
ON MOST LIGHTWEIGHT
MULTI-SPEED BIKES.
SINGLE-SPEEDS HAVE
COASTER BRAKES.

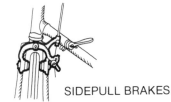

CENTERPULL BRAKES

SIDEPULL BRAKES

You steer a bicycle by turning the handlebars and shifting your weight as you go around a corner. The handlebars are attached to the front wheel by a fork and stem. The stem passes through a headset with bearings so the whole system can turn freely.

THE BICYCLE AND ITS PARTS

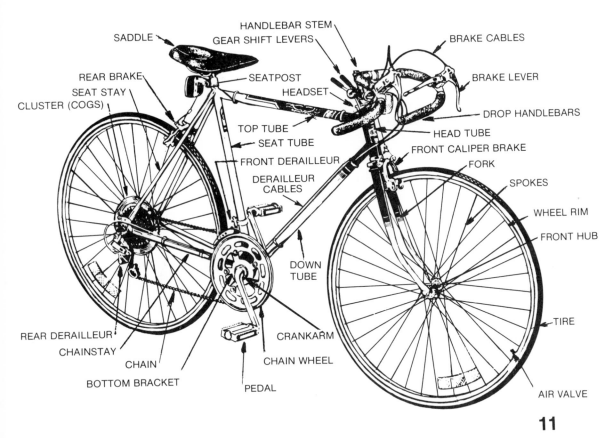

SADDLE
HANDLEBAR STEM
GEAR SHIFT LEVERS
BRAKE CABLES
REAR BRAKE
SEAT STAY
CLUSTER (COGS)
SEATPOST
HEADSET
BRAKE LEVER
DROP HANDLEBARS
TOP TUBE
SEAT TUBE
HEAD TUBE
FRONT CALIPER BRAKE
FRONT DERAILLEUR
FORK
DERAILLEUR
CABLES
SPOKES
WHEEL RIM
FRONT HUB
DOWN
TUBE
REAR DERAILLEUR
CHAINSTAY
CHAIN
BOTTOM BRACKET
CRANKARM
CHAIN WHEEL
PEDAL
TIRE
AIR VALVE

11

There are two main types of handlebars: upright and drop (racing) style. Upright bars let you sit upright on the seat. They are used mostly on children's bicycles and utility bikes, including three-speeds. Many children's bikes have highrise bars similar to uprights but taller.

Most lightweight bicycles have drop handlebars. They let the rider lean forward to put more power into each stroke of the pedals. There are drop handlebars designed differently for touring and racing. If you have drop handlebars on your bicycle, *don't turn them upside down*. That makes the brakes hard to reach, which can be dangerous. If you want to ride upright, have upright bars put on your bicycle.

SADDLES

RACING
(BMX BIKES
USE ONE OF
THE RACING TYPES)

TOURING STYLE
(WIDER THAN
RACING STYLE)

UTILITY
(MATTRESS)

The kind of saddle you have on your bicycle is very important, especially if you ride long distances at a time. Although a bicycle comes with one kind of saddle, you can put on a different type if you wish. Most bikes with upright handlebars have wide "mattress" saddles with springs for a smooth ride. Good racing-style saddles are narrow and made of leather that shapes itself to the rider. Many lightweight bikes have hard plastic seats that are only *shaped* like racing or touring saddles. Although they are all right for short rides, they are uncomfortable on long ones. "Banana" seats are long saddles found on children's bikes with highrise handlebars.

The kind of wheels your bicycle has depends on the type of bike it is, what it is designed for, and how much money it cost. Some have heavy steel wheels with wide "balloon" tires. Other wheels are made of lightweight alloy with thin high-pressure tires. "Mag" wheels with steel or plastic spokes and wide thick-tread tires are used mostly for dirt racing.

TIRES

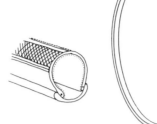
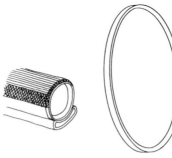

CLINCHER OR WIRED-ON TIRES
USED ON MOST UTILITY, CHILDREN'S,
AND TOURING BIKES.

TUBULAR OR SEW-UP TIRES ARE
USED PRIMARILY ON RACING BICYCLES.

Full-sized, multi-gear bicycles such as 10- or 12-speeds have one of two kinds of tires: clinchers or sew-ups. Clinchers (wired-ons) are found on almost all factory bicycles. They have a separate tube and come in several widths depending on the size of your wheel rim. Sew-ups (tubulars) are primarily for racing and have a tube sewn into the tire itself. The whole thing is glued to the wheel rim. Sew-ups are generally too thin and delicate for lots of road use. They are better suited to track racing, although some cyclists use them for touring.

PEDALS

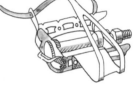

RUBBER TREAD PEDAL FOUND
ON UTILITY AND CHILDREN'S
BIKES.

RACING PEDAL WITH TEETH TO
GRIP FOOT. (ON TRACK AND BMX
BIKES, ALSO.)

ROAD AND TOURING
PEDAL COMMON ON
MULTI-SPEED BIKES.

Pedals also differ according to the kind of bike you have. Utility and children's bikes usually have rubber-tread pedals. Racing bikes, including BMX (bicycle moto-cross), have lightweight pedals with teeth to grip the rider's shoe. Lightweight multi-speed road bikes have a pedal similar to the racing type, but usually without teeth.

Both racing and road pedals are called "rat-traps" and are designed so toe clips can be used with them. Toe clips and straps hold your foot in place so you pull up on the pedal as well as push down on it. More advanced riders use toe clips to get the most out of their muscles and to keep their feet from slipping off the pedals.

13

Multi-speed bicycles have different gears to help you go uphill with less effort and downhill without having to pedal as fast as you would on a single-speed. Multi-speed bicycles have more than one cog in the rear and may have two or three chain wheels in front. A bike with one chain wheel and five cogs is a five-speed. A 10-speed bicycle has five cogs in the rear and two chain wheels, so there are 10 possible chain wheel/cog combinations, or 10 speeds. A 12-speed has two chain wheels and six cogs; a 15-speed has three chain wheels and five cogs. There are even 18- and 21-speed bicycles with three chain wheels and six or seven cogs.

SHIFT LEVERS

FINGER-TIP SHIFTER   STEM-MOUNTED SHIFTER   DOWN-TUBE SHIFTER

The chain on a multi-speed bicycle is moved or "derailed" from one position to another by a metal "derailleur." There is one derailleur in the rear for the cogs and one in the front if there is more than one chain wheel. The levers that operate the derailleurs are usually on the bicycle downtube, the handlebar stem, or at the very ends of the handlebars.

A three-speed bicycle is different. There is no derailleur and each gear is in a set position on the hand lever that changes gears inside the rear hub.

Types of Bicycles

At first all bicycles were single-speeds. In many countries of the world people still do most of their traveling on one-speed utility bicycles. They carry farm animals to market, and in Mexico once we saw a family of five riding to town on

CRUISER (BALLOON TIRE)

one bicycle. Such bicycles have steel frames designed to carry heavy loads, upright handlebars, mattress saddles, and wide clincher tires that work well on rough roads. Many children's bicycles are small models of adult utility single-speeds. There are three- and five-speed utility bicycles also.

Touring bicycles are designed for comfort, with longer frames and low gears for hill-climbing. They may have 10, 12, 15, 18, or 21 speeds (gears). Touring bicycles usually have drop handlebars so the rider has several places to put his or her hands during long hours on the bike. Wheels are lightweight but strong, with heavy-gauge spokes and durable clincher tires. Touring saddles are wider and more comfortable than racing saddles. A touring bicycle has toe clips, water bottles in holders on the frame, racks with panniers (saddlebags) for carrying gear, and a tire pump for flats. There may be fenders and lights for traveling at night.

WOMAN'S OR GIRL'S BICYCLE — POPULAR WITH WOMEN WHO FEEL UNCOMFORTABLE ON A MAN'S FRAME. GIRLS OR WOMEN SHOULD FIND THE FRAME SIZE THEY NEED BY STRADDLING A MAN'S OR BOY'S BIKE THEN BUYING THAT SAME SIZE FRAME IN A MIXTE-STYLE OR GIRL'S BIKE. BUT THERE IS NO REAL REASON WHY WOMEN AND GIRLS CANNOT RIDE MEN'S FRAME BICYCLES. IT IS USUALLY A MATTER OF BECOMING USED TO IT.

15

Racing bicycles are the lightest bikes made. Their shorter frames give a hard ride but make the bike easy to manage. They have from 10 to 21 speeds but do not have the very low gears found on touring bicycles. Although all 10-speeds are often called racing bikes, most are too heavy and not designed for racing. Racing handlebars are narrower and deeper than touring bars. Wheels are built for speed rather than strength, with lightweight sew-up tires. Track-racing bikes have no brakes or gears and weigh as little as 15 pounds. A touring bike weighs about 28 pounds, and a utility bike weighs 35 pounds or more. Road-racing bikes have brakes and gears but nothing extra, such as fenders, kickstands, water bottles, or tire pumps.

A new style of bicycle that looks much like bikes did back in 1950 is gaining popularity with many people. These balloon-tire old-style bikes are called "mountain bikes," "cruisers," or "backroad bikes." You can buy a brand new "old" bike just about anywhere, and there are clubs and special races just for them. They are used for really rough riding on dirt roads and trails. Some are single-speeds, but some have the full range of gears found on touring bikes.

BMX bikes, used either for dirt-racing or street-riding, are popular with young people. True BMX bikes are built for rough use and jumping on dirt tracks. Many children's bikes are made to look like BMX bikes, but they are not built for that kind of rough use. Make sure your bike *is* if you jump curbs or ride off paved roads.

BMX BICYCLES ARE USED FOR TRICK RIDING AND JUST PLAIN FUN. ERIK WILHELM PUTS HIS LIGHTWEIGHT 3-SPEED BMX BIKE THROUGH SOME TRICKS AT HIS HOME IN COLORADO. *(Photo by Tim Wilhelm)*

(Photo courtesy of Bicycling Magazine, Rodale Press, Inc., Emmaus, PA)

3 | WHEN YOU BUY A BICYCLE

The first thing to decide when you want a new bicycle is how you are going to use it. Do you want it for riding to school and around the neighborhood? Do you want to do dirt-riding and curb-jumping with your friends? Will you take it out on all-day rides or overnight trips with your family? Are you growing so fast that you will need another bike next year? Your answers to these questions will help you decide what kind of bicycle you need. Don't just buy whatever is popular.

Where should you buy your bicycle? If you are growing fast or don't want to spend much money, you may find a good used bike at a garage sale or through a newspaper ad. Take an adult with you who knows bicycles, or you may end up with a bad bike that costs more in the long run than a new one. Department and discount stores have new inexpensive bicycles. But you may not be able to buy parts when you need to, and most do not repair the bicycles they sell. Many are of such poor quality that they do not last more than a year.

The best place to buy a bike that will last is at a bicycle shop. Bicycles are complicated and need service or repair now and then. The salesperson at a bicycle shop knows about bikes and will be there to help even after you take it home. Their better bicycles have replaceable parts that can change with you over the years.

19

PROPER FIT:
TO DETERMINE THE CORRECT
FRAME SIZE FOR YOU,
STRADDLE BIKE WITH ABOUT
1″ TO SPARE IN THE CROTCH
ABOVE BAR.

Bicycles come in many sizes and shapes. They go by frame size *and* wheel size. There are bikes with 16-inch wheels for small children, 20-inch wheels on BMX or banana-seat bikes for older children, 24-inch wheels on multi-speed bikes for bigger children, and full-sized bikes with 26- or 27-inch wheels.

When you are ready for a full-sized 26- or 27-inch wheel bike, you also need the correct frame size. Adult bikes range in frame size from 19 to 25 inches (the distance between the center of the bottom bracket and the top of the seat tube). To find out which size you need, the salesperson will have you straddle a boy's bike, even if you will be buying a girl's or Mixte frame. You should clear the top tube by no more than one and one-half inches. Be sure to wear the shoes you will use when riding when you size a frame. That will be the frame size you need in any bike with that same size wheel.

Bicycle prices depend on what the frame is made of and what components (parts) are on the bike. If you are fully grown, it is better to buy a good frame—even if it has poor components. You can replace the saddle, handlebars, wheels, even the gears later as you can afford better ones. If you are still growing, buy a less expensive frame with good components that you can put on a larger, better frame when you reach your full growth.

Once you have your new bike, let the shop adjust the seat height, but watch how they do it so you will be able to do it yourself. To find the right height, sit on the saddle with your *heel* on the pedal at its lowest point; your leg and knee should be *straight*, not bent. Then, still sitting on the saddle, put the *ball of your foot* over the center of the pedal—still at its lowest position—and your knee should be *slightly bent*. A saddle that is too high or too low is uncomfortable, dangerous, and will make your legs get tired much sooner.

When you adjust the saddle on any bike, make sure you never raise it so high that there is less than two inches of seat post still in the frame tube. If you need your saddle higher than that, your whole bike is too small for you.

THE CORRECT RIDING POSITION:

A.) THE FIRST STEP TO DETERMINE THE RIGHT SADDLE HEIGHT IS TO SIT WITH YOUR HEEL ON PEDAL WITH YOUR LEG FULLY EXTENDED.

B.) THE SECOND STEP IS TO PLACE THE BALL OF YOUR FOOT IN THE RIGHT POSITION ON THE PEDAL WITH YOUR LEG SLIGHTLY BENT AT THE KNEE.

Have the people at the bike shop make sure all the parts of your bike fit properly. Then you will ride better and farther without getting sore and tired. The handlebars should be at the right distance from the saddle, not too high or low. Make sure your hands fit the brake levers also.

What else do you need once you have your new bicycle? A tire patch kit and a set of tire irons are necessary to repair flats. Many bicycle repair books tell you how. As you learn to take care of your own bike, you might want to buy other tools to fit your seat, handlebars, brakes, and derailleurs. When you go for long rides, you should carry a small hand air pump for your tires. If you don't and have to fill your tires at a gas station, be careful not to blow them up too far. A friend of ours accidentally blew up both tires with a gas station air pump and ended up walking all the way home.

Besides tools, you may want a basket or rack to carry things. Be sure that the rack you buy fits your particular bike. Some people carry items in a handlebar bag; others prefer panniers or wire baskets that fold up when not in use. When we shop for groceries, we use a bike trailer. Although most of them cost almost as much as another bicycle, they soon pay for themselves by not having to drive the car every time we shop. We use our Pelican trailer for overnight camping trips, since it has a waterproof lid and holds all our camping gear.

As you get more serious about cycling, you will want a water bottle for those long hot trips. When riding at night, you need a light to see the road and to let others see you. Your new bike will have legal reflectors on the front, the rear, on each pedal, and on the wheels. Put reflectors on your old bike if they are missing.

Another thing you need for cycling is a helmet. Most bike riders who die in accidents die from serious head injuries. Wearing a helmet is not only safe, it is smart. Automobile drivers take you more seriously because you *look* more serious in a helmet. Bicycles are not toys, and you help people realize that by wearing proper head gear. Helmets may seem expensive at first, but one helmet is a lot less expensive than one head injury.

Finally, you need a good lock for your bike. The best are U-shaped pieces of hardened metal that weigh almost two pounds but are thief-proof. If you don't want to carry one of those, use a thick cable or chain. Make sure the lock is just as good as the cable itself. Always lock your bike to something that can't be moved, such as a railing or a post. Put the cable through both wheels and the frame too; otherwise you may return to find only one wheel locked to the rack.

HOW TO LOCK YOUR BICYCLE

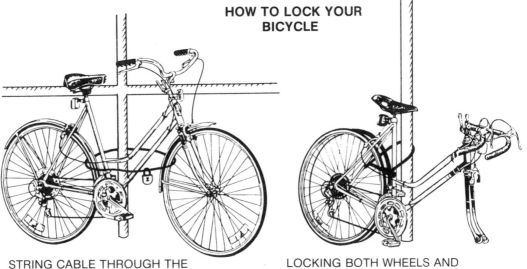

STRING CABLE THROUGH THE WHEELS AND FRAME TO MAKE SURE THAT BIKE IS LOCKED TO SECURE OBJECT.

LOCKING BOTH WHEELS AND FRAME BY REMOVING FRONT WHEEL AND USING U-SHAPED OR CITADEL-TYPE LOCK.

If you keep your bicycle clean and lubricated, it will last for years. There are many books to help you learn how. Some are listed under the heading Learning More in Chapter 6. If you don't like to work on your bike, ask the bike shop people when you should bring it back for a checkup. A good bike shop will help you keep your new bike in good working order, so that when you are ready to ride, your bike will be too.

4 | LEARNING TO RIDE A BICYCLE

If you don't know how to ride a bicycle, now is a good time to learn. Take your bike to a paved area, such as an empty parking lot, a schoolyard, or a quiet street. Lower your saddle so your feet touch the ground (or almost). Now, push yourself along with both feet and see how far you can coast each time without touching the ground. Keep at it until you feel ready to try pedaling.

You can have someone hold your bike as you begin to pedal or you can do it alone. Keep your saddle low so you can balance yourself with both feet. Now, push off and coast as before, but this time put your feet on the pedals and give them a turn. If you start to fall, put your feet back on the ground for a second. Each time you will be able to pedal a little longer. Do not start out by running and throwing your leg up over the saddle. It is easier to straddle the bike and push off with one pedal each time. That is how professional cyclists do it.

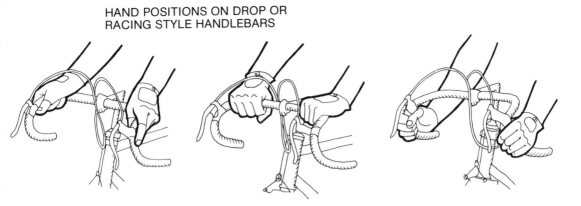

Once you can pedal and balance, raise your saddle to the right height. Now you are ready to work on skills that will make you a *good* rider. The first thing you need to learn is how to stop correctly. What kind of brakes does your bike have? If they are coaster brakes, just pedal "backward." Your pedals will stop and so will your bike.

If you have hand brakes, squeeze each lever to see which one works the front and which the rear brake. On most bikes (not all), the right lever works the rear brake; the left lever works the front brake. Just remember, Right = Rear.

Practice using your brakes in a parking lot or a place where there is no traffic. Slowly squeeze the rear brake first, then both together. Most of the stopping force is in the front brake; squeeze it firmly but gently so you won't be thrown over the handlebars. Practice using your brakes correctly, so it will become a habit you don't have to think about.

The first time you ride a bike with drop handlebars it may feel strange, even scary. Practice riding with your hands in different places on the bars and use the brakes in each hand position so you can brake quickly when you need to.

It is hard to look behind you when you ride with drop handlebars. Instead of twisting your head to look *over* your shoulder, duck your head to look back *around* your shoulder. That will keep your bike traveling in a straight line. Otherwise your bike will swing out into the road. Serious cyclists use a small rearview mirror attached to their sunglasses or helmet to see behind them. You can buy one at your bike shop for a few dollars.

25

Practice riding in a straight line, turning, stopping, starting, and balancing while pedaling slowly. Develop your cycling skill for riding in the real world by riding painted lines in a parking lot or schoolyard until you can do it without wobbling, even with one hand on the handlebars. You need to learn to ride with one hand so the other is free for turn signals. *Never* carry something in one hand while you ride. Use both hands to brake and control your bike except when signaling.

Once you master basic riding skills, you may want to work on other skills that will help you ride like a professional. *Cadence* describes how fast and steadily you pedal. It is very tiring to pedal hard, then coast and rest, yet most beginning cyclists do just that. Try to pedal from 60 to 70 times per minute. To find out what your cadence is, count each time your right knee comes up as you pedal for one full minute. By using lower gears and pedaling faster, you travel much farther without getting tired. As you learn to shift properly, try to keep up the same cadence even when climbing or going down hills.

Using toe clips is another skill to develop as you gain experience. You can add toe clips to rat-trap pedals whenever you wish. Toe clips hold your foot in the right position and don't let it slip. They also help you pull up on the pedal instead of only pushing down. This doubles your power with each stroke of the pedal. When you first use toe clips, take off the leather straps. Ride without them until you can pull your foot straight back out of the clip each time you stop. Flip the clip up with your toe as you start out and slide your foot in smoothly. When you put the straps on, don't cinch them up so tight that you can't easily slip your foot in and out. It doesn't take long to learn to use toe clips. In fact, you may wonder how you ever rode without them for so long.

Learning to shift correctly is complicated but necessary to becoming a skilled bike rider. On a three-speed, shifting is easy. Put the lever at the number of the gear you want.

Low gear is No. 1, or L, middle or normal gear is No. 2, or N, and high gear is No. 3, or H. Low gear helps you go up hills, and high gear helps you go faster or downhill. You can shift a three-speed without pedaling at the same time.

On bikes with derailleurs there is no set position for each gear, and *you must always pedal as you shift*. First, learn which hand lever operates which derailleur and how. With the rear wheel off the ground, work the shifters and watch how the derailleurs move the chain from one cog or chain wheel to another. Each position is a different gear. You are in lower gears when the chain is closest to the bike, higher gears as it moves farther away. It is best not to ride with your chain on the closest chain wheel *and* farthest cog, or on the farthest chain wheel *and* closest cog. This puts a lot of stress on the chain and causes parts to wear out faster.

Once you see how your gears operate, take your bike to a parking lot and practice shifting through each gear combination until you get the feel of it. Be sure to shift as you pedal so you don't jam the derailleurs. To get the most out of your gears, shift *before* you really need to. You will feel the pedals get really hard to push or really easy when it is *past* time to shift.

Learning to be a good cyclist means taking care of your bicycle's engine—your body. It does no good to have a great bike with the latest gear if your body wears out before you get where you want to go. Cyclists need plenty of good food before riding, especially fruit and starchy foods like cereals and breads. High protein foods, such as cheese, meat, and eggs take longer to digest and don't give instant energy while you ride. But you need them afterward to build and repair your body.

Getting enough sleep helps you to be a better cyclist, and cycling helps you to sleep better.   Riding a bicycle takes more muscular skill and control than driving an automobile or flying an airplane. Give your body all the help it needs by eating, sleeping, and rejecting things that will be harmful.

27

COMMON SIGNS SEEN FOR BICYCLING

5 | RIDING IN THE REAL WORLD

To ride in the real world you need to follow the same rules that apply to automobile drivers. Your bicycle is not a toy. You can get a ticket if you break a law on your bike, and you may even have to pay a fine. But safety is the most important reason to follow the rules. Most bicycle accidents happen to children between the ages of five and fifteen. Learn the rules and follow them so you will be a responsible and safe rider.

The most important rule is to *ride on the right*. You must *never* ride facing traffic. Drivers do not expect a cyclist to be coming at them from that side of the road, especially if they are turning left into a driveway or at an intersection.

You are supposed to ride as far to the right as *practical*, so don't ride in a gutter or where there is broken glass or gravel at the side of the road. *Don't weave in and out* of cars parked along the right side. It is better to ride in a straight line along the right side of traffic than to weave in and out so that drivers don't know where you will be next. Watch out for someone opening the door of a parked car as you ride by.

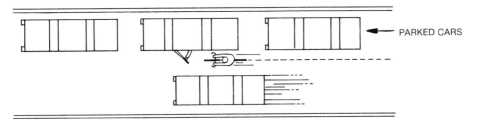

DO NOT RIDE SO FAR TO THE RIGHT THAT YOU MIGHT HIT AN OPENING CAR DOOR.

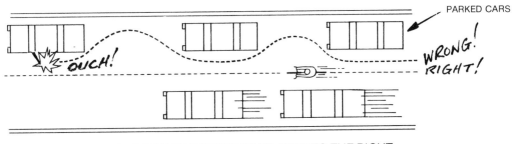

DO NOT ZIG-ZAG THROUGH PARKED CARS. RIDE TO THE RIGHT OF MOVING TRAFFIC, BUT NOT SO FAR AS TO BE DANGEROUS.

Obey all traffic signs when riding your bicycle. Come to a complete stop at all Stop signs, yield to other vehicles at Yield signs, go slowly in a Caution zone, and follow signs that direct traffic to the left or right. It may seem silly to stop at a Stop sign, especially when there is no traffic coming or when your friends zoom on through. But it is the law. Laws are made so everyone will be safe and will know what to expect from other people.

Watch out for people who are walking across the street. You must stop for them just as you do in an automobile. *Never ride your bike on a sidewalk.* Warn people with your voice or a bell if they don't see you, but be ready to stop if you must.

Watch at intersections for drivers who may turn in front of you. Many don't see bicycles or think you are going slower than you are. Use your ears to listen for cars passing or pulling out close to you. Never ride with earphones on that keep you from hearing what is going on around you.

29

When you park your bike, be careful not to block a sidewalk or entrance to a building. Store owners don't like bikes placed where customers may trip and get hurt. If you are courteous and considerate on your bicycle, people will treat you like the responsible person you are.

If there is a separate bike path, use it, but be careful when it ends, especially at a street or intersection. Watch for people on the bike path who might be walking their dog on a leash. The dog could run in front of you and get tangled in your bike wheels. Walk your bike and avoid the risk of getting hurt or hurting someone else.

There are two ways to make a left turn. One way—the safest if traffic is heavy—is to ride on the right side through the intersection *with* the green light, then get off your bike and walk across the street *with* the green light going the other way. If traffic is not heavy and as you become a better rider, make a left turn just as automobiles do. Signal first so drivers know what you are going to do, then pull over into the left-turn lane. Signal again, then with *both* hands on your handlebars, make the turn with the green light.

LEFT TURNS

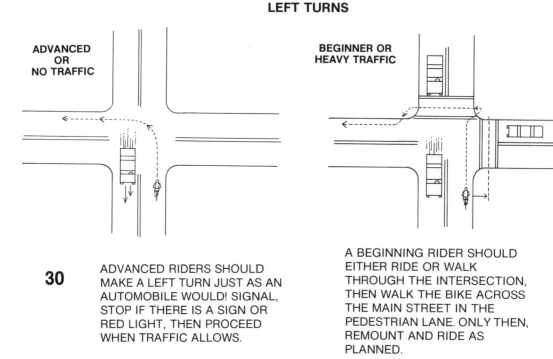

ADVANCED OR NO TRAFFIC

BEGINNER OR HEAVY TRAFFIC

30 ADVANCED RIDERS SHOULD MAKE A LEFT TURN JUST AS AN AUTOMOBILE WOULD! SIGNAL, STOP IF THERE IS A SIGN OR RED LIGHT, THEN PROCEED WHEN TRAFFIC ALLOWS.

A BEGINNING RIDER SHOULD EITHER RIDE OR WALK THROUGH THE INTERSECTION, THEN WALK THE BIKE ACROSS THE MAIN STREET IN THE PEDESTRIAN LANE. ONLY THEN, REMOUNT AND RIDE AS PLANNED.

It is fun to ride with friends, but dangerous if you don't keep your mind on the road. *Ride single file* unless you are on a bike path; even then you should if bikes are coming the other way. Don't carry anyone else on your bike unless it is made to do so. *Never* hold on to a moving vehicle to "hitch a ride." It is very dangerous and not too smart.

Your best protection when riding in the real world is to *be seen*. The first thing a driver says after a car/bicycle accident is, "But I didn't see him!" Wear bright clothing when you bicycle; red or yellow is best. A bike flag that rises above car level helps drivers know you are there. Wear a helmet both to protect your head and let drivers know you are a serious cyclist. Make sure your bike has all legal reflectors, and use bright-colored panniers when you carry things.

Make *eye contact* with drivers around you. Look them "right in the eye" so you can tell if they *really* see you before you pull out in front of them. Use *hand signals* to tell drivers if you are stopping, or turning right or left. Signal before you make a turn, look at drivers to make sure they see you, then use both hands on the handlebars to make the turn itself.

As you ride, be careful of open drains or grates. Your bike wheel can get caught in one, making you "take a header." Lightweight bicycle wheels are not made to jump curbs or ride over broken paving and rocks, but don't swerve into traffic to miss bad places on the road. Stop and walk through the problem rather than risking a flat tire, broken wheel, or collision with traffic.

For some reason dogs love to chase bicycles. Most stop once they get very far from their home territory. Others stop if you shout "No!" or "Stay!" at them. Some cyclists get off their bike and keep it between them and the dog while waiting for the dog's owner. Whatever you do, try not to show fear or get off your bike and run. You will be able to pedal away from most dogs without any special problem.

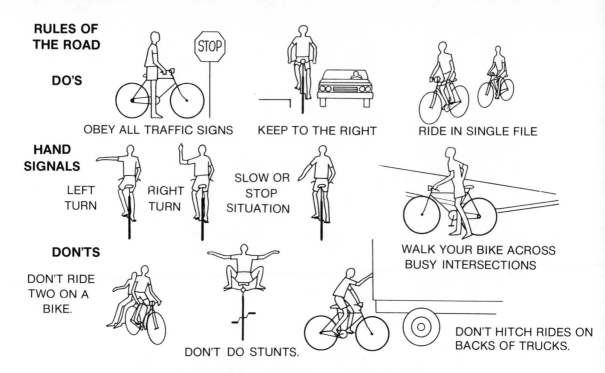

RULES OF THE ROAD

DO'S

OBEY ALL TRAFFIC SIGNS   KEEP TO THE RIGHT   RIDE IN SINGLE FILE

HAND SIGNALS

LEFT TURN   RIGHT TURN   SLOW OR STOP SITUATION

WALK YOUR BIKE ACROSS BUSY INTERSECTIONS

DON'TS

DON'T RIDE TWO ON A BIKE.

DON'T DO STUNTS.

DON'T HITCH RIDES ON BACKS OF TRUCKS.

No amount of safety precaution will help if your bike itself is unsafe. Check your bike each time you go for a ride.

1. Spin your TIRES looking for nails or glass that might cause a flat. Squeeze each to make sure it has air or use an air pressure gauge if you have one.
2. Squeeze each brake lever to make sure your BRAKES work. If you have coaster brakes, hop on and test them.
3. Twist the HANDLEBARS to make sure they are not loose.
4. Wiggle the SADDLE to see if it is tight and doesn't twist sideways.
5. Wiggle the SPOKES two at a time to see if any are broken.
6. Make sure nothing is HANGING LOOSE to get caught in your wheels.

If your bike hasn't had a checkup at the bike shop in a long time, take it in to be oiled, greased, and tuned up. As long as you take care of your bike, it will take you where you want to go.

RIDING WITH A BIKE CLUB MAKES A DAY SPENT ON YOUR BICYCLE EVEN MORE FUN.

(Photo courtesy of Bicycling Magazine, Rodale Press, Inc., Emmaus, PA.)

6 | AS YOU IMPROVE

As you get better and want to ride more, you might like to join a cycling club. Ask at your local bike shop whether there are any in your area. Most clubs have regular rides on weekends and special rides at other times of the year. If you can't find a club to join or aren't old enough to ride with a club in your neighborhood, start one of your own with friends.

Cycling clubs sometimes have "Novice Rides" for beginners. Otherwise, you should be able to ride at least 10 miles nonstop before you try to ride with a club. Even then, know what a ride is like before you start out. A 10-mile ride through steep hills can be harder than a 20-mile ride over gentle country.

Before you join a club ride, check your bike to see if it is in good working order. Take along water and food unless there are planned eating stops. Others in the group will probably have tools and tire pumps, but it is a good idea to have your own if you plan to ride regularly.

Learn the habits of the club you ride with. Do they welcome newcomers? (Most do!) Do they have voice or hand signals to warn of glass or other problems on the road? Do they ride hard and fast, stopping to rest only after a "good workout," or do they ride slowly with lots of stops to talk and sightsee? Will there be others your age? Do they have different riding groups for different ability levels? Ask all of these questions and you will be more sure of finding a group to match your own ability and wants.

Many cyclists and club riders plan their vacations around cycling. You may want to also. All over the United States, especially during spring and summer, cycling groups hold exciting rides open to anyone who wants to join. One of the most famous is TOSRV, Tour of the Scioto River Valley, a two-day 210-mile ride in Ohio. Another is RAGBRAI, the Register's Annual Great Bike Ride Across Iowa. One of the great Western biking events is a hard all-day ride from Tecate to Ensenada, Mexico.

Some groups sponsor "century" rides: 100 miles in one day—usually within 12 hours. Sometimes new riders think a century is impossible until they find themselves in good shape and actually doing it one sunny day. So many have done centuries that a "double century"—200 miles in 24 hours—is becoming the challenge that a century used to be.

If you would like to ride a century in six months or a year from now, start to train right now. Ride an hour each day as hard and fast as you can, then on weekends go for distance. Work gradually up to 25 miles a day, then 50, 60, 70. Once you are able to ride 50 to 70 miles in less than seven hours, you can probably do a century in 9 to 12 hours.

Drink lots of fluids on a century ride. Your body needs water before your thirst knows it. Have someone follow or meet you at certain points with snacks and to help with bike repairs if needed. Some official century rides give a shoulder patch afterwards to show you did it. But if you go out, work at it, and do a century all by yourself, *you* will know you did it and *that* is the most important thing.

Whether you decide to take off on a bicycle tour, get into racing, ride a century, or just use your bike wherever and whenever you want, you may want more information. Here are some organizations to write, some magazines to read, and books that will help you enjoy bicycling even more.

Learning More

Organizations:

American Youth Hostels
National Campus
Delaplane, VA 22025

Bikecentennial
P.O. Box 8308
Missoula, MT 59807

League of American Wheelmen
P.O. Box 988
Baltimore, MD 21203

Canadian Cycling Association
333 River Road
Vanier, ON K1L 8B9

Magazines:

Bicycling
33 East Minor Street
Emmaus, PA 18049

American Wheelmen
League of American Wheelmen (see above)
members only (write to the league)

Books:

Ballantine, Richard. *Richard's Bicycle Book*, Ballantine Books, 1978.

DeLong, Fred. *DeLong's Guide to Bicycles & Bicycling*, Chilton Book Co., 1978.

Hawkins, Karen and Gary. *Bicycle Touring in the Western United States*, Pantheon Books, 1982.

Wilhelm, Tim and Glenda. *The Bicycle Touring Book*, Rodale Press, 1980.

Racing:

United States Cycling
Federation
1750 E. Boulder St. #4
Colorado Springs, CO 80909

BMX Action Magazine
Bicycle Motocross Action
P.O. Box 5277
Torrance, CA 90510

THE PROPERLY LOADED BICYCLE
READY FOR TOURING

FOAM PAD

SLEEPING BAG

TENT

WEIGHT OF LOADS SHOULD BE DISTRIBUTED OVER FRONT AND REAR WHEELS. HEAVIEST ITEMS ARE PLACED ON FRONT OF THE REAR RACK, NEAR THE FRAME AND TO THE BOTTOM AND INSIDE OF THE PACKS.

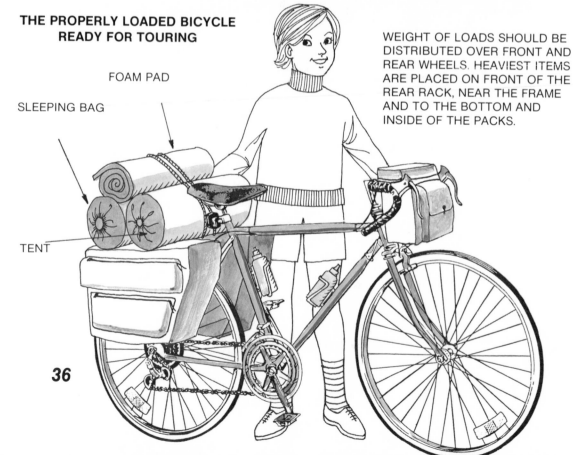

VERMONT BICYCLE TOURING ENCOURAGES CHILDREN TO TOUR WITH THEIR FAMILIES AND OFFERS A WIDE VARIETY OF TRIPS THAT RANGE FROM EASY TO DIFFICULT. *(To find out more about bicycle tours in Vermont write Box 711, Bristol, VT 05443 for a free catalog.)*

7 | BICYCLE TOURING

You are bicycle touring when you ride your bicycle on an all-day or overnight trip, or one that lasts many days. Cyclists tour the world on everything from single-speed heavy-duty bicycles to multi-speed lightweights and tandems.

In 1975 our family of four rode bikes 3,000 miles from the Pacific Ocean to the Atlantic near Washington, D.C. Kirsten, our daughter, was just nine years old. She rode a 24-inch 10-speed and was the youngest person to ride across the country on a bicycle. The trip was a summer vacation, and we camped out most of the way. We rode about 50 miles a day and had plenty of time left to swim and sightsee. Our two-year-old son rode along in a bike trailer.

More recently, thousands of people have ridden across the United States on Bikecentennial's TransAmerica Trail, established in 1976 to celebrate our country's 200th birthday. You can get maps, tour guides, and other useful cycling information by joining Bikecentennial. Their address is listed under the heading Learning More in Chapter 6.

The best place to begin bicycle touring is at your own front door. Is there a distant park or favorite swimming place you would like to visit? Do you have friends or relatives to go see on the other side of town or in the country? Is there some museum or art gallery you have been wanting to visit?

Before you take off for a day-trip or longer, there are some things you need to think about and do. First, decide where you want to go. That will depend on how far you can cycle without getting too tired. You should be able to ride 10 miles without stopping, before you try an all-day tour. Fifty miles in one day is about the most many cyclists like to travel, unless they are in super shape and traveling light. A day-tour to a lake or park 10 to 15 miles away with a picnic, a swim, and the return ride is about right for most first tours.

Go with a friend or family on your first tour. You will have more fun and if anything goes wrong, you will have help. Be sure your friends are good riders and know the rules of the road. Plan the trip together. Planning is almost as much fun as the trip itself.

Decide ahead of time which route to take. You may be able to use bike trails part or all of the way. We like to take circle tours that begin and end at home so we don't backtrack. You don't have to pick some super special place to tour. Part of the fun of touring is noticing all the things you miss otherwise.

Take food and water on your bike tours. Biking is hard work, and you need to drink and eat snacks along the way. We stop every hour for about 10 minutes, just to stretch our muscles, have a piece of fruit or some nuts, take a drink of water, and look around. It is better to stop and snack often than to ride for hours, then eat a big meal.

Carry your food, spare jacket, basic tools, and anything else you need *on your bike* rather than on your back. If you don't have panniers, strap a day-pack or bag to your rear rack. Be sure nothing is hanging loose to get caught in your spokes. If you don't have a bike rack, load a small day-pack lightly to carry on your back, but tie it around your chest with an extra strap so it won't slip as you ride. Once you are touring regularly, you will want some basic gear, such as panniers, tire pump, water bottle, handlebar bag, and perhaps a lightweight sleeping bag for bike camping trips.

MAKE SURE YOU ARE PREPARED FOR ANY KIND OF WEATHER WHEN BICYCLE TOURING. A HELMET AND WATER BOTTLE ARE IMPORTANT TOURING GEAR. *(Photo by Tim Wilhelm)*

When you can spend a whole day on your bicycle without being too sore the next day, you can try an overnight tour. Stay with some friends, plan a trip with your family to a motel, or camp out. The main difference between an overnight and a day trip is having to get on your bike and ride that second day. Keep your first such trip short, because the second day seems longer and harder than the first.

When you bike-tour, always be prepared for a change in the weather. A warm sunny day may turn into a cold rainstorm that can ruin your trip if you are not prepared. Short pants are more comfortable while bike-touring, but we always carry a pair of long pants for colder weather, sightseeing, or just lying around camp at night.

If you are interested in touring with a commercial group, check ads carefully in the cycling and outdoors magazines. Some tours cost as much or more than any other kind of vacation, while others are minimum trips where you cook and carry your own food and camp out in public places. Check age limits on any tour you hope to join by yourself or with your family. Some welcome youths along, while others insist you be accompanied by parents, and some are for adults only.

Whether you someday want to tour Vermont in the autumn, the Grand Canyon on a balmy spring day, the Pacific Coast in midsummer, or the Appalachian Mountains during a school break, start bicycle touring right now from your own front door. You just may decide that it is the very best way to see your world.

(L-R) MIKE GOEDDY, TOM CHRISTOPHER, AND KELLY McDOUGALL ARE THREE THIRTEEN-YEAR-OLDS WHO HAVE BECOME VERY INVOLVED IN BMX RACING. *(Photo by Bob Osborn, BMX Action Magazine)*

8 | BICYCLE RACING

Bicycle racing began as soon as there were bicycles. It is becoming more popular today in America and is a regular event in the Olympic Games. In 1984 there will be a women's Olympic bike race for the first time.

There are four basic categories of bike racing: time trials, set distance, road races, and track racing. In TIME TRIALS riders race for their best time, usually on a set road course. Many bike clubs and groups sponsor time trials for their members or anyone who wants to join in. MASSED START races are where all riders start together and ride a set course. The first one across the finish line is the winner. CRITERIUMS are short races over roads closed off to other traffic. STAGE races are timed over several days with the rider having the best time each day taking the lead. CYCLO-CROSS races, becoming more popular in America, cover courses that include fences, streams, mud, sand, and woods. Some people travel all over the country to take part in off-road races like the one held each year at Crested Butte, Colorado.

THESE RIDERS ARE WAITING FOR THE NEXT TRACK RACE; THEIR TRACK BIKES HAVE NO BRAKES OR GEARS TO SHIFT, BUT THE RIDER IN THE MIDDLE NEEDS A SMALLER BIKE FOR MAXIMUM EFFICIENCY AND SAFETY. *(Photo courtesy of Bicycling Magazine, Rodale Press, Inc., Emmaus, PA)*

The Tour de France is the most famous road race in bicycle racing. It takes 22 days and covers 3,000 miles. People in Europe know more about it than most people in America know about the Super Bowl.

If you are interested in bike racing, start in your own neighborhood. Check at your local bike shop for racing clubs in your area. Your city or town might have scheduled races during the year. If you can't find organized races, race against yourself and the clock. Set up a route and try to beat your own time. Use a stopwatch or a watch with a second hand, and keep track of your best times. Then compare your performance with official racers records available at the library or in cycling magazines.

At first the kind of bike you ride is not too important. If you get serious about racing, you will need a racing bike with special components and racing gears.

To ride in "sanctioned" (official) races, you must join the United States Cycling Federation. Write them (see Learning More, Chapter 6) for an application form and information on races near you. You might be our next Junior National Champion.

One of the hard things to learn in bike-racing is how to ride in a "peloton" (tight pack) without bumping or wrecking. Experienced racers ride fast within a few inches of each other's wheels. They "draft" behind the front riders, letting them break the wind so they can go fast with less effort. Strategy—learning how to position yourself during a race—can mean the difference between winning and losing. The only way to learn pack-riding, drafting, and strategy is by riding with experienced racers.

Most racers work out every day with one day off a week. Interval training is off-and-on-again effort, such as riding 10 miles at an easy pace, then 10 hard miles, and so on. Some racers do intervals, others ride hard one day and easy the next.

BMX racing started in California and spread all over the country. Most racers are from eight to eighteen years old, and it is popular with both boys and girls. All you need to start is a BMX bike, a helmet, a good strong body, and a track.

BMX race tracks are as simple as a back lot where kids have some jumps and turns in hard-packed dirt, or an official course maintained by a BMX organization. A good track has large and small jumps along the "esses" (right and left turns), "whoop-de-doos" (round bumps close together), and "berms" (banked turns).

Besides a BMX helmet, racers wear long pants and shirts with padding at the knees and elbows for "endos" (crashes). High-topped rubber-soled shoes protect ankles and keep feet from slipping.

BMX bikes are strong reinforced 20-inch bikes with special wheels and components. Even full-grown riders use the small bikes. Motocross racing is rough on bikes, so they must be cared for constantly.

If you are interested in BMX racing, see if there is an organization near you. If not, gather some friends, lay out a track, and start a BMX group in your neighborhood. There are BMX magazines that will tell you all about how to start.

BIKES OF THE FUTURE MIGHT BE PEDALED BY BOTH HANDS AND FEET. *(Photo courtesy of Bicycling Magazine, Rodale Press, Inc., Emmaus, PA)*

9 | CYCLING IN THE FUTURE

For too long the bicycle has been thought of as a toy. We are so used to using a car to go anywhere—even just a few blocks to the store—that we don't think about the huge waste of energy. Eighty percent of all automobile traffic is within eight miles of home, a distance easily covered by bicycle. Equipment such as racks, panniers, and trailers make hauling packages and even small children easy.

Today some businesses encourage workers to use bicycles to get to work. They provide lockers and showers for their bike commuters. Eighteen bicycles can be parked in the space needed for one automobile. Thirty bikes can ride in the road space needed by one moving car. Many cities are hoping that bicycles will solve some of their traffic problems in the future.

Still, people don't ride bikes to work or shopping as much as they could, because they are too slow or because of bad weather. Both of these problems may be solved by the bicycles of the future. Every year at the Human-Powered Speed Championships in California, bicycles that hardly look like bikes, with rocketlike coverings, travel at speeds up to 60 miles per hour. These bikes are designed mainly for speed, and the riders are in excellent physical condition. But now that they have proven how fast they can regularly go, the designers are working harder to make the bikes practical for road-riding by anyone.

The bicycle of the future may be a "recumbent," a bike that lets the rider sit back much as he or she would in an automobile. Recumbent owners today say their bikes are more comfortable than regular bikes, go faster, and are easier to manage in city traffic. Some have pedals for both the feet *and* the hands, others have three or four wheels, and some take more than one rider.

It is hard to build a bike that protects the rider from the weather, yet is light enough to be pedaled easily. Covers make the bike hard to balance and steer. But many people are working to invent a bicycle good enough to replace the automobile for all short trips and many long ones.

Even though the basic design of bicycles has not changed much in 100 years, a lot of people are thinking about how to make them even better. Bicycles will change because our world and our needs are changing. The bicycle of the future may be one that is already going 55 miles per hour at the Human-Powered Speed Championships. Or it may be one getting a new aerodynamic shell in someone's garage workshop right now. The spirit of the Wright brothers is still at work and will bring us the bicycle of the future, maybe sooner than we think.

GLOSSARY OF TERMS

Alloy: a substance made of two or more metals mixed together for strength.

Axle: a rod on which the wheel turns.

BMX: bicycle motocross—it is both a type of bicycle and a style of racing.

Bottom bracket: the cylinder located down at the base of the pedals and crank arms that is made up of an axle, fixed cup, adjusting cup, lock ring, and ball bearings.

Brake pad: the rubber block on a caliper brake that presses against the rim of the wheel to stop it.

Cadence: the number of times the pedals are turned per minute.

Cage: the metal part of the derailleur that guides the chain.

Caliper brakes: using metal arms and brake pads to ''pinch'' the wheel to a stop. They are operated by hand levers connected to the brake arms with cables.

Century: a 100-mile bike ride completed in under 12 hours.

Chain: a series of metal links that connect the drive mechanism of the bicycle.

Chain wheel: a metal disc with teeth that hold the chain. It is located at the base of the pedals and crank arms; there may be more than one on a multi-speed bike.

Clinchers: a common name for wired-on tires. They are held on the wheel rim by pressure against a nylon (or wire) bead around the edge of the tire.

Cluster: the group of cogs ''clustered'' at the rear wheel axle; sometimes called a freewheel.

Coaster brakes: operated by pushing backward on the pedals.

Cog: a metal disc with teeth that hold the chain, located at the axle of the rear wheel. If there is more than one, the set is called a cluster.

Components: the parts of a bicycle.

Crank arms (cranks): the metal ''arms'' that hold the pedals and turn the chain wheel.

Criterium: short road race on a course closed to other traffic.

Cyclocross: a race through rough back-country where you may have to carry your bike part of the way over fences, through mud, or across streams.

Derailleur: the lever, cable, and metal cage device that moves the chain from one chain wheel or cog to another.

Disc brakes: using a metal disc at the rear wheel axle. Brake pads squeeze the disc instead of the wheel rim to stop the bike.

Double century: a 200-mile bike ride completed in less than 24 hours.

Down tube: the frame tube that runs from the bottom of the handlebars to the bottom bracket.

Draft: to ride behind another cyclist so closely that he or she acts as a wind break for you, allowing you to ride equally fast with much less effort.

Fork: the tubular portion of the frame that holds the front wheel.

Frame: the main structure of a bicycle. It is made of lightweight tubing.

Freewheel: the part of the rear wheel axle mechanism that lets the wheel turn even when the rider is not pedaling.

Handlebars: the metal tube that the cyclist holds and uses to control the bike.

Headset: the bearing mechanism located on the front fork that lets the front wheel turn separately from the rest of the bicycle.

Hub: the center part of a bicycle wheel to which the spokes attach and through which the axle runs.

Interval training: a type of physical conditioning using hard then easier effort.

Massed start: a race where all the riders begin together at the starting line.

Mixte frame: a bicycle frame with a dropped top tube for riding by someone wearing restricting clothing, or someone who does not like the higher top tube arrangement.

Panniers: saddlebags used on a bicycle to carry gear.

Peloton: a group of racers riding in a tight pack.

Rat-traps: metal pedals made with holes and slots for toe clips and straps.

Recumbent: a bicycle that lets the rider sit back as in an automobile.

Reflectors: devices that shine brightly to let people, especially drivers, see the cyclist. By law they must be located in several places on each bike.

Rim: the metal outer part of a bicycle wheel that holds the tire and spokes.

Sanctioned race: an official bike race approved by the U.S. Cycling Federation.

Seat tube: the frame tube extending from under the seat down to the bottom bracket.

Shifters: the levers that work the cables running to the derailleurs. Used to shift gears, they can be located on the ends of the handlebars (fingertip shifters), on the stem, or on the down tube.

Spokes: long, thin pieces of metal that are laced from the hub to the rim in a bicycle wheel.

Stem (gooseneck): the bottom part of the handlebar section that hooks into the steering tube and headset.

Tandem: a bicycle built for two riders.

Time trial: a bike race against the clock where the rider tries to beat his or her own best time.

Tire iron: a small metal lever device used to remove and replace clincher tires.

Toe clips: metal ''cages'' that attach to the pedals and hold the rider's feet in place. They are usually used with leather straps that go over and around the foot.

Top tube: the frame tube that extends from the handlebar area back to the seat on a diamond-frame (boy's) bicycle.

INDEX

DATE DUE

OCT 2 4			
MAY 1 0			